ONE TINY
SEED

Brenda Jason

To my parents, Don and Karen, who provided a firm foundation of faith and encouraged me to reach for the stars; to my husband, Jim, who helps keep my feet on that firm ground as I reach; and to my daughter, Kaylyn, who has taught me more than I expected about God's love and grace.

Introduction

If you have problems with your faith, you are not alone. Even the disciples, who left everything and spent three years with Jesus had difficulty believing. Jesus rebuked them many times for doubting His glory and His power and questioning the ministry He was sent to do.

"If that is how God clothes the grass of the field, which is here today and tomorrow is thrown into the fire, will he not much more clothe you – you of little faith?"
~ Matthew 6:30 (NIV)

"You of little faith, why are you so afraid?"
~ Matthew 8:26 (NIV)

"Immediately Jesus reached out his hand and caught him. 'You of little faith,' he replied, 'why did you doubt?'"
~Matthew 14:31 (NIV)

"Aware of their discussion, Jesus asked, 'You of little faith why are you talking among yourselves about having no bread?'"
~ Matthew 16:8 (NIV)

The fact is: Jesus spent more time addressing the disciples lack of faith than He did encouraging them for expressing any faith.

In Matthew 17:20 (NIV), Jesus said, *"Because you have so little faith. Truly I say to you, if you have faith as small as a mustard seed, you can say to this mountain, 'Move from here to there,' and it will move. Nothing will be impossible for you."*

The mustard seed is only about 1/64th of inch. It is one of the smallest seeds that produces a tree; yet the trees can grow up to 20 feet tall and 20 feet wide. The mustard tree is found in various locations throughout the world. It can thrive in arid, dry climates, in cool, wet climates and can even grow in sandy and clay soil. The mustard tree can also be cut down to the trunk and then grow back again. For the believer, it should be an encouragement that Jesus compares our little faith to the tiny mustard seed.

Our faith is often tested in the dry climates, the fiery trials that might include being planted in clay or sandy soil, rather than perfect ground. We will often be stretched to grow through the cool, wet climates, when the floods of life's circumstances appear to have us in water over our heads. When we feel like life's bottom has dropped out or we have been cut down to nothing, we are reminded that new growth can come through pruning. It is in the pruning that the tree comes back larger and stronger than ever. And so it is for faith, the growth and pruning of our faith, yields a greater harvest, a more faithful servant.

And it all begins with one tiny seed. One tiny seed of faith – planted and nurtured by God in the climate and soil of His choosing. He chooses how much water, how much sunshine and what nutrients are needed for growth. He may even uproot and transplant the tree, or chop it down to its trunk to encourage greater growth. God alone can take the tiniest seed of faith planted in your heart and, at His appointed time, He will provide the abundant harvest of what you need just when you need it. May this small devotional be just the seed you need to plant today for tomorrow's harvest.

Saving Faith

*For by grace you have been saved through
faith, and that not of yourselves;
it is the gift of God.* ~ Ephesians 2:8

The gift of God is salvation *by* grace *through*
faith. It is a gift freely offered by God to all
who are utterly unworthy of it, but who, on
the basis of the gospel message, receive
God's gift of salvation. What is the gospel
message? Quite simply, that while we were
yet sinners, God demonstrated His own love
toward us by sending His only begotten Son
to be born among us, live with us, die for us,
rise above us and return to His heavenly
throne beside God to reign in us.

But knowing this about Jesus is not enough,
or even believing He is the Son of God does
not guarantee your salvation. Even the
unclean spirits know He is the Son of God
and still refuse to turn from evil (Mark 3:11).
The gospel message begins with the
acknowledgement that you are a sinner who
admits you have fallen short of God's
expectation, His plan for you as the pinnacle
of all His creation, and that you are destined
for eternal death, if not for the saving work of
Christ.

Being a good person cannot save you. There
are no works you can do in your own
strength, in your flesh, that will provide this
gift to you. The gift is given when you agree

with God to turn from your sinful ways, confess with your mouth that Jesus is Lord and believe in your heart that God has raised Him from the dead. You can only be saved by confessing your sins and placing your faith in God's Son, Jesus Christ, the Lamb of God, who died and paid for all your sins on the cross. It is through His shed blood, that salvation is possible.

Romans 10:13 says, "whoever calls on the name of the Lord shall be saved." God promises that to all who receive Jesus as the Lord of their lives, "to them He gave the right to become children of God, to those who believe in His name: who were born, not of blood, nor of the will of the flesh, not of the will of man, but of God" (John 1:12-13). To those who welcome Jesus as Lord, their lives are reborn spiritually, they receive new life, eternal life, from God. Through Christ, this new birth begins to change you from the inside out – molding your behavior, transforming your mind, and conforming your character into the image of Christ.

If you have not received God's gift of salvation, will you reach out, speak up and choose to turn from your sin? If so, just say this simple prayer: "God, I know that I have sinned against you and am deserving of punishment. But Jesus Christ took the punishment I deserve so that, through faith in Him, I could be forgiven. With your help, I give my life to You. Thank you, Father, for this gift of eternal life. In Jesus' name I pray. Amen!"

If this prayer was not a new prayer to you and you have already received God's gift of salvation before today, give prayerful thought to areas of your life you may have compromised or not yet yielded to God's work. Then commit to surrender them to Him today in prayer, asking God's Holy Spirit to help you change.

Martin Luther said, "God our Father has made all things depend on faith so that whoever has faith will have everything, and whoever does not have faith will have nothing." God's desire is that you would live the Christian life abundantly (John 10:10). Doing so requires you to feed your faith with the Word of God, talk to your Creator every day in praise and prayer, exercise your faith in action by obeying His instructions, and share your faith with others. When you do these things, He will enter your lives with immeasurable power.

Now that you have committed your life to Christ, and all areas of it, begin by reading Psalm 100 out loud!

Psalm 100: A Song of Praise for the Lord's Faithfulness to His People

^{1} Make a joyful shout to the Lord,
all you lands!

^{2} Serve the Lord with gladness;
Come before His presence with singing.

^{3} Know that the Lord, He *is* God;
It is He *who* has made us,

and not we ourselves;
We are His people and
the sheep of His pasture.

⁴ Enter into His gates with thanksgiving,
And into His courts with praise.
Be thankful to Him,
and bless His name.

⁵ For the Lord *is* good;
His mercy *is* everlasting,
And His truth *endures* to all generations.

When you enter His presence with praise,
He enters your circumstances with power!

Day 1

Called by Name, Created for Glory

But now, thus says the Lord, who created
you, O Jacob, And He who formed you, O
Israel: "Fear not, for I have redeemed you;
I have called you by your name;
You are Mine. When you pass through the
waters, I will be with you; And through the
rivers, they shall not overflow you. When
you walk through the fire, you shall not be
burned, Nor shall the flame scorch you.
Everyone who is called by My name, Whom
I have created for My glory; I have formed
him, yes, I have made him.
~ Isaiah 43:1, 2, 7

All too often, we try to define ourselves or attain our identity through titles and roles, status or position, wealth and fame, or through appearances and other standards the world thrusts on us. But through His prophet Isaiah, God reminds us, "… I have redeemed you, I have called you by your name; You are Mine … I have created [you] for My glory; I have formed *you*, yes, I have made *you*" (vv. 1, 7). Here God declares, we are not only designed by Him, as He has created formed and made us; but He is also our redeemer, as His only begotten Son purchased each one of us with His blood on the cross (Ephesians 1:7).

In the original language the three verbs in Isaiah 43:7: created, formed and made, describe the process of formation from the first rough cutting to the perfecting of the work! Even before time began as you were formed in the womb – God has already fashioned all your days and written them in a book and the work He does as He forms you is accomplished with a plan to finish the work He began in you (Philippians 1:6).

From these verses we know not only who we are, but whose we are – we belong to a loving Creator and He remains with us as His plan for us gloriously unfolds. He calls each of us by our name, He is with us in the midst of the storms, protecting us through fiery trials and giving all that is needed to gather His beloved back into His arms. Our God is continually saving us!

The references to water and fire in verse 2 are pictures of hardship. *Waters* is a general term. *River* is a specific term. *Fire* is a general term. *Flame* is a specific term. God is with you in your specific trials – not just through a year or a month or a day, but in an hour, in a minute, in a second. At every precise moment in time, God is with you! Do you trust Him with your circumstances, or are you too busy wondering, "How deep is the water?" "How long can I keep my feet on the bottom?" "How long can I tread water?" Do you trust that God has His hand on the thermostat, and that He is with you in the fire? Will you stay in the fire long enough for the sacrifice to be made into ash? Do you trust God to then make beauty from the ashes?

> *…To give them beauty for ashes,*
> *The oil of joy for mourning,*

The garment of praise for the
spirit of heaviness;
That they may be called
trees of righteousness,
The planting of the Lord,
that He may be glorified.
~ Isaiah 61:3

Lord, teach me to let go,
until my heart is filled with peace
and I learn to know Your will!

Rivers of Living Water

He who believes in Me, as the Scripture has said, out of his heart will flow rivers of living water. ~ John 7:38

The original Greek language indicates that Jesus *shouted* these words *with passion* to all who would hear. It was a particularly daring proclamation to make on the final day of the Feast of Tabernacles when no water was ceremoniously drawn from the Pool of Siloam for the offering. Jewish tradition identified the pool as the Messiah's Pool and it was the only source of fresh water within the walls of Jerusalem. To proclaim that He provided all the water a person needed, when the crowd was thirsty, drew murmuring and unbelief from the crowd and hostility from the Pharisees.

While Jesus had previously used the words "living water" in John 4:10 to indicate eternal life, here again His promise was not for the physical water they longed for, but rather for the spiritual water of the Holy Spirit. By proclaiming He had this water, the people knew He was claiming to be the promised Messiah. To give the Holy Spirit to all who believed was something only the Messiah could do (Isaiah 12:2-3, 44:3-4).

The term, *out of his heart*, literally means *out of his belly*. The point is that living water will flow out of your innermost being, your heart, soul, spirit. To say that it will *flow* means you do not just get a single drink, but you get a spring, a fountain, a well. You get Jesus and all His power and the source of that drink will never leave you. Jesus knows His followers need to remember this promise; as He knows what lies ahead and does not want your faith shaken or destroyed. Only the ever flowing power of the Holy Spirit can quench your disbelief.

To what extent do rivers of living water flow from you? This is a question that both convicts and brings hope to the believer. It convicts us of our barren walk with Jesus. If we are honest, none of us would say Jesus' words describe our lives completely! Honesty, instead forces us to say, "Well, there's been a trickle of living water, but some droughts too. Occasionally, there has been a tiny little creek of living water running. But always flowing, abundant *rivers*? Oh, Lord, yes, please help me!"

Jesus' words give us hope. "He who believes in Me …" The promise comes when you come to the Son of God and drink, when you quench your thirst with the life giving power only He can give. Then, and only through Him, will rivers of living water flow out of your innermost being. Make this your daily prayer and become a vessel of His immeasurable power with rivers of living water flowing from you.

The power of faith reflects the immeasurable power of God. ~ Lisa Spivey

Day 3

See the Glory

Then Jesus said to her, "Did I not say to you that if you would believe you would see the glory of God?" ~ John 11:40

Lazarus is sick. His sisters, Martha and Mary, send for Jesus. Though Jesus loved this family, He delayed going to them for two days. He knew Lazarus would be dead by the time He and the disciples arrived, but He had a greater plan. Martha's, Mary's and the disciples' desire to see Lazarus healed would be surpassed by God's plan to raise him from the dead. In John 11:4, Jesus told them, "This sickness is not unto death, but for the glory of God, that the Son of God may be glorified through it."

Imagine what the disciples must have thought when Jesus then told them Lazarus was dead as they set out to go to him two days later. He had promised them his sickness was not leading to death, but as they set out toward Judea they hear he is dead. Certainly doubt and confusion filled their thoughts. They knew Jesus was capable of healing the sick. They had seen His miracles. Why would Jesus have denied Lazarus healing?

After arriving, as Jesus comforts Martha and Mary, He wept. The original language indicates He made audible sounds while gasping deeply. How comforting to know our Savior knows the pain of our losses and empathizes with us. His knowledge of the future did not keep Him from mourning with those He loves. He mourns with you too when you lose a loved one. Or maybe you have lost a job, a home, a plan for your future? Has it been difficult to see God glorified through these circumstances? Has your heart become hard like stone over the loss?

By the time Jesus reached his friends, Lazarus had been in the tomb for four days. A stone had been rolled over the entrance to keep the stench of death inside. We, too, can roll a stone over our heart, keeping our own stench of death inside when we experience loss. Graciously, Jesus says, "Take away the stone..." (John 11:39). He alone has the power to roll away the stone over our own hearts. And as He did with Lazarus, He then commands His purpose to come forth.

Corrie Ten Boon said, "Never be afraid to trust an unknown future to a known God."[1] Martha, Mary and the disciples were looking for God to demonstrate His glory in ways known to them, rather than allowing God to glorify Himself as He intended. His delay in going to Lazarus had a specific purpose. God's timing, especially His delays, may make us think He is not answering or is not answering the way we want Him to answer. But He will meet all your needs according to His perfect schedule and purpose (Philippians 4:19). The prophet Isaiah reminds us God's ways are not our ways, and His thoughts are higher than our thoughts (Isaiah 55:8-9). His knowledge and wisdom are far greater than man's. We are foolish to try to fit God into our molds – to make His plans and purposes conform to ours. Instead we must strive to follow His plans and purpose for our lives. And that requires that we believe we will indeed see the glory of God when the stone is rolled away!

Lord teach us to glorify You through our faithfulness!

Day 4

Amazed Beyond Measure

Then He went up into the boat to them, and
the wind ceased. And they were greatly
amazed in themselves beyond measure,
and marveled. ~ Mark 6:51

After sending the disciples to the west shore of the sea by boat, Jesus went up the mountain to pray. Separated from their Master, having rowed for hours against a contrary wind and strong waves, the disciples were physically drained. Their physical struggle and painful attempt to make headway through the storm was a picture of their spiritual struggle in trying to understand who Jesus really was. They understood Jesus had power, but did not yet understand Jesus was power.

Even in the midst of the storm, the seasoned sailors were not in a panic until the sight of someone walking on the water came toward them. The original language of the text states the sight of the presence caused them to shriek in terror, believing they were seeing a ghost. The Apostle Mark records that Jesus came to them with the intention of passing by them. He intended to let His entire divine glory pass by the disciples, just as God had done for Moses when he wanted assurance of God's presence with him (Exodus 33:22).

Immediately Jesus speaks words to both comfort them and encourage them. "Take courage! It is I [literally I AM]; do not be afraid" (Matthew 14:27). Hearing the Savior, but still filled with doubt, Peter challenges, "Lord, if it is You, command me to come to You on the water." Jesus simply replies, "Come." With his eyes now fixed on Jesus and his heart swelling in obedience, Peter leaves the boat and the other disciples and walks on the water. But as quickly as he does, he realizes he is doing the impossible and as his eyes move from Jesus to the waves, he sinks. When his eyes move, his faith sinks quickly, and all he can do is cry out to Jesus, "Lord, save me."

Just as God did with Moses, He presents Himself as a God of mercy and compassion and plucks Peter from the water and sets him safely back in the boat. He then climbs into the boat with the disciples and immediately the storm stopped and the boat was at the other side, back in safe harbor. The disciples were absolutely astonished and awakened to who Jesus was and all He had been teaching them. The event was an epiphany for the disciples as they finally understood Jesus' deity. They now realized they were following the Son of God and this miracle proved that God himself had visited them in the flesh. The only response they have is to worship Him as they moved from fear to faith, from confusion to confession, from wondering to worshiping.

Peter's personal experience was like the psalmist who said, "When I said my foot

slips, Your mercy, O Lord, held me up"
(Psalm 94:18, AKJV). Like Peter, when our
faith slips, God is there, and declares if you
are Mine, you are safe. We can keep trusting
God in the direst of circumstances, in our
most hopeless moments, regardless of how
strong the storm rages around us. As
Augustine said, "He came walking on the
waves; and so he puts all the swelling storms
of life under his feet. Christians, why be
afraid?"

*You can never cross the ocean until you
have the courage to lose sight of the shore.
~ Christopher Columbus*

Day 5

Power to Effect Change

*For whatever is born of God overcomes the
world. And this is the victory that has
overcome the world – our faith.* ~ 1 John 5:4

John begins with a principle that is so simple,
yet so powerful – whatever is born of God
overcomes the world. If you are born of God,
you will overcome the world. In other words,
anything born of God cannot be defeated by
anything (or anyone) of the world. In 1 John
4:4, we are reminded that as children of God
we can overcome the lies, confusion and
chaos brought on by the world. We can do
this because He who is in us is greater than
he who is in this world. All too often we lose
sight of this truth. We lose sight because our
faith is not built on the rock of our salvation
(faith in Christ), but rather quick moving
sand that ebbs and flows with the tides of life.
We lose sight because we do not place our
trust in and reliance upon the Holy Spirit to
guide   us   through   the   temporary
circumstances that come with living in this
world.

The key to victory is faith. Not only an initial,
"come to Jesus and be saved" faith, but a
consistently   abiding   faith,   an   ongoing
reliance and trust in the work of Jesus Christ.
Faith is the cause of victory, the means, the
instrument, the spiritual armor and artillery
by which we overcome. Faith works by love
to God and Christ, and as it does its work it

removes us from the pressures and temptations of the world. Faith sanctifies our heart, and purifies it from the lusts of this world. The strength of our faith comes from the Son of God, who said, "In this world you will have tribulation, but be of good cheer [take courage], I have overcome the world" (John 16:33).

There is nothing that can hinder you. Even when it seems odds are against you, you can take hold of the promise of Jesus that He has overcome the world. Jesus Christ – the One who overcame the world, the One who dealt with every temptation successfully (Hebrews 4:15), the One who stared down the enemy (Matthew 4:1-11) – lives in every believer by the power of the Holy Spirit and through Him lies victory (John 16:13-14). You may be in the midst of the battle, but it is your faith that makes you a conqueror and gives you certain victory.

C. H. Spurgeon notes, "Look at any Greek lexicon you like, and you will find that the word faith [or believe] does not merely mean to believe, but to trust, to confide in, to commit to, entrust with, and so forth; the very marrow of the meaning of faith is confidence in, reliance upon."[2] By faith, you have the power to effect whatever change God is asking you to make when you place your confidence in and your reliance upon the Holy Spirit who dwells in you (John 16:13-14). When you are surrendered to God's work in you through the battle, then by the power of the Holy Spirit, you will have the power to effect change whether it is to increase your own faith or that of a lost and dying world who so desperately needs faith in Jesus. Sweet child of God, the continuous victory is yours ... keep on conquering!

Christians, by all means believe that Jesus has obtained for you the power to overcome the world and its deep, hidden seductions to love for ourselves. Believe this. Believe in Him as Victor and you also will have the victory. ~ Andrew Murray

Day 6

Rewards Await the Faithful

But without faith it is impossible to please
Him, for he who comes to God must believe
that He is, and that He is a rewarder of
those who diligently seek Him.
~ Hebrews 11:6

There is a familiar worldly saying, "Seeing is believing," but in spiritual matters that is not necessarily true. Not all who saw Jesus' miracles in person believed in Him, nor do all today who read the eyewitness accounts of Jesus' miracles in the Gospels believe in Him. Contrary to the world's understanding, God says, "Believing is seeing." In spiritual matters faith precedes understanding. It is faith that opens our eyes to God and then, subsequently, a desire to know Him and therefore, please Him.

The only thing that makes it difficult for us to see and believe is our own human will. As a Christian, your will must be to seek Him from a place of pure devotion. Empty words, repetitive prayers or chants, or ritualistic practices do not please God (Isaiah 1:11, Matthew 6:7). No number of good works can compensate for your lack of faith (Ephesians 2:8-9). God will not settle for a mere acknowledgement of His existence. He desires a personal, dynamic relationship with you that will transform your life.

Chapter 11 of the Book of Hebrews is often called the Hall of Faith. Here the triumphs and trials, exploits and endurance of many Old Testament believers is revisited. We see faith subdue kingdoms, open wombs, close the mouths of lions, quench fires, make men and women courageous in battle, and take down giants with a single, small stone. In the New Testament faith forces demons to run, compels the lame to walk, the dumb to speak, the deaf to hear, the dead to rise, the fearful to walk on water, and the timid and awkward to preach Christ. Each victory has one thing in common. All those involved were seeking to worship God diligently and were subsequently rewarded by their desire to know God and to please Him. Yet how do our lives compare with theirs?

Faith is the only thing that gives God His proper place, and puts man in his place too.[3] Amazingly, God's response as we seek to glorify Him is to reward us. The Greek word for *rewarder* (*misthapodótēs*) means one who is paid wages, "by *someone* paying what is due; or by a *paymaster* giving rewards in keeping with *his own values*." Our diligence [faithfulness] in seeking God will earn us tangible wages, visible rewards – in accordance to God's riches – the hope of heaven and the blessings of Christ-like growth while we journey from here to there.

Pastor Max Lucado says, "God honors radical, risk-taking faith. When arks are built, lives are saved. When soldiers march, Jerichos tumble. When staffs are raised, seas still open. When a lunch is shared, thousands

are fed. And when a garment is touched –
whether by the hand of an anemic woman in
Galilee or by the prayers of a beggar in
Bangladesh – Jesus stops. So make your
choice, announce your faith to God, and
demonstrate your devotion."[4]

*And those who know Your name will put
their trust in You; For You, Lord, have not
forsaken those who seek You. ~ Psalm 9:10*

Faith in the Darkness

*Fear not, for I am with you; Be not
dismayed, for I am your God. I will
strengthen you, Yes, I will help you, I will
uphold you with My righteous right hand.*
~ Isaiah 41:10

Fear and faith have one thing in common.
They both ask us to believe in something we
cannot see. Faith asks us to look with eyes
that will behold the glory of God, but often
fear convinces us to foresee anxiety and
worry as we look into what we perceive to be
darkness. God intends us to look toward the
light, but Satan is determined to cast shadows
over us. It is difficult to trust what we cannot
see, and so we turn toward idols to satisfy our
immediate need, whatever it may be.

Habakkuk 2:18 warns us that the idols we
carve profit us nothing and are teachers of
lies. Yet when trials come, our tendency is to
trust in other people, in money, in position,
status or titles, or in the strength of our own
flesh to deliver us through our circumstances
and away from our enemy. We stare into
what we believe is overwhelming darkness
and try to bring our own light to the
circumstances. We trust in the idols our
hands have made, and therefore in our own
power as creator and sustainer. If we say we
trust God but put our trust in our bank

account, home, business or in other people or comforts, then we are idolaters.

Yet even in our disobedience, God so tenderly asks, "Have idols ever cared for you so tenderly? Can they strengthen you and uphold you and bring you to a righteous place? Do they remain with you, or do they take their leave as soon as the moment passes? How long will you contend in the darkness before you realize that I am with you, yes, even there, I will help you?"

What a beautiful promise God has given each of us in Isaiah 41:10! We are assured of His presence, His relationship, His help and His sustaining power. To have faith is to trust God beyond what the eyes cannot see or the ears do not hear. To have faith is to trust in the Holy Spirit and not the emotions brought by the circumstances. Faith looks towards God's blessings, which are not always easy, painless, simple, comfortable or expected. Sometimes a blessing comes wrapped in the mystery of divine darkness.

But be reminded – from dark clouds we get precious water; from dark mines we get valuable jewels, and from our darkest trials God offers redemption through His only begotten Son born in the dark of the night. You need not fear because God is with you, He is ever present, all sufficient ("I am with you"), He has established a relationship with you ("I am your God"), and He gives you assurance of His strength, help and victory over sin and death and your daily circumstances. He has not forgotten you, nor will He forsake you (Deuteronomy 31:6). Do you acknowledge all the ways God helps you on a daily basis? Be reminded – God is with you always, to the very end of the age (Matthew 28:20).

I have learned that faith means trusting in advance what will only make sense in reverse. ~ Philip Yancey

Day 8

Chosen and Set

*I have chosen the way of faithfulness; I have
set my heart on your laws.*
~ Psalm 119:30 (NIV)

No one wanders into holiness or comes by it
without sweat and sacrifice. It requires a
deliberate determination to walk in truth and
purity. C. H. Spurgeon said, "The commands
of God must be set before us as the mark to
aim at, the model to work by, and the road to
walk *in*." To say the road to walk *in*, means
something quite different than the road to
walk *on*. When we are "in" something, we are
devoted to it, put effort toward it, and make
sacrifices for it. To choose the way of
faithfulness requires we set our hearts on
God's commands and walk *in* them in
obedience.

The Hebrew word used for "chosen" implies
the one doing the choosing is aware they are
choosing the choicest, select or desired way,
because it is what is required, but also
because experience has proved it is truly the
best way. It is the same Hebrew word used in
Joshua 24:15, when he declares he and his
household will choose to serve the Lord and
Jesus later uses the word in Luke 10:42 when
he admonishes Martha, telling her, Mary has
chosen the better part.

The word "set" means we will be sure-footed, or established because the path will be laid out smooth or even, and that as it is laid out as such, we will be made fit or worthy, and will be brought into agreement with or resemblance to that which we are pursuing. When we set our hearts to pursue faithfulness, God, according to His laws, will provide the path. The false assumption we often make is that what God declares as the smooth, even path will be one without danger or trial, or without any difficulty or sacrifice.

"I have set" implies that you will not be moved because your heart is set on God's laws. The only way this can happen is if you first choose to be faithful. However, faithfulness does not exempt you from the day-to-day circumstances of life. Believers and unbelievers alike experience pain, trouble, and failure at times (Matthew 5:45). To be set means your heart is established, because you desire God's way, His Word, over all the other choices, and by experience, His way has been tried and proved to be the best despite the outcome and regardless of your expectations. This is the path of faithfulness for everyone who declares themselves a disciple of Christ.

We often assume the disciples were men of great faith from the first time they met Jesus. This is not true! If it were true, Jesus would have had no need to beckon them more than once to follow Him (Matthew 4:18-22, Mark 1:16-20, Luke 5:1-11, John 1:35-42). Though it took time for Jesus' call and His message to get through, the disciples followed, but once they set their hearts to follow Jesus, they had to grow in their faith just as we all do (John 14 and John 20). As we obey, our faith increases and as our faith increase so does our desire to obey. But don't ask God to guide your footsteps if you are not first willing to move your feet!

Faith is not belief without truth, but trust without reservation. ~ D. Elton Trueblood

Faith Bears Fruit

*Thus also faith by itself, if it does not have
works, is dead.* ~ James 2:17

James declares that genuine faith and good
works are inseparable. Works are not the root
of salvation but the fruit of salvation, they are
not the cause but they are the effect. Calvin
said it simply, "We are saved by faith alone,
but not by a faith that is alone."[5] If there is
faith and no works, then the faith is dead. By
the same measure, it does not mean that we
earn our salvation by serving and obeying
God, but rather that such action demonstrates
our commitment to God. Works of loving
service are not a substitution for our faith, but
instead a verification of our love and faith in
Jesus Christ.

False faith or intellectual faith is an
incomplete faith that is inadequate to produce
the good works demonstrated by the renewed
heart of a sinner. Those with genuine faith act
based on the transformation of their conduct
and thoughts. Genuine faith always results in
a changed life and fruit that bears the Holy
Spirit's works of love, joy, peace, patience,
kindness, goodness, faithfulness, gentleness,
and self-control in us and through us
(Galatians 5:22-23). The fruit of the Spirit is
the by-product of a life bound with Christ. If
we want the fruit to grow in us, we must join

our lives to Christ, abide in Him, and He in us (John 15:4-5).

Earlier James asked, "What does it profit, my brethren, if someone says he has faith but does not have works? Can faith save him?" (James 2:14). Jesus had voiced a similar warning when he told his disciples many will call Him "Lord, Lord" but will not enter heaven because He never knew them (Matthew 7:15-23). According to this warning, there will be many who believe they have done things in Jesus name, whose works will be rejected on judgment day. Paul confirms this in 1 Corinthians 3:13 when he cautions that the quality of our works will be tried by fire. There is no provision for the quantity of works, only the quality.

Jesus call us to examine our motives. He never emphasized external signs of genuineness. He demanded inward commitment to God's will, which in turn produces the good fruit of a changed life. He is not asking what have you done *for* me, but rather, what will you do *with* me? Will you come to me and allow your inner attitudes and outer behavior to be absolutely transformed? Or will you continue trying to add faith in God onto your life and asking God to bless your own ambitions and pursuits? True faith in God changes who we are and what we do from the inside out. The fruit from these changes is not produced by us but by the Holy Spirit in us and through us. It is never work we can accomplish in our own strength.

Though we belong to God's Kingdom while we are still here on earth, true faith changes our priorities in work and play, in relationships and commitments, in service and stewardship. Genuine faith gives birth to works with Kingdom results that demonstrate the fruit of the Holy Spirit in us.

Everything that God does begins with a seed and ends with a harvest!

Faith's Perfect Work

*. . . knowing that the testing of your faith
produces patience.* ~ James 1:3

Trials are part of life. James tells us they are
inevitable. We know this because he states
"... *when* you face trials," not *if* you face
trials, "count it all joy, knowing that the
testing of your faith produces patience" (1:2-
3). This is not a "don't worry, be happy, it's
okay to stick your head in the sand until the
trial goes away" encouragement, but rather
practical and realistic advice to allow the
trials that hit us to produce patience. Why?
Because when patience is allowed to perfect
its work in us, we will be made complete,
lacking nothing (v. 4). The point is not to
pretend to be happy when we face trials, but
to *choose* a heavenly attitude because of what
the trials can produce in our lives. As a
believer, true faith chooses to respond with
joy when it faces testing, knowing the testing
will produce patience.

The word *knowing*, means that we cling to the
truths in God's Word and know by personal
experience, and subsequently, remember
what godliness came from previous trials. It
carries with it the implication that we are
certain each trial will stand up to the test and
that God is using the trials for His purpose.
God is not unaware of our circumstances.
Scripture is clear that He is sovereign over all

things. He causes the sun to rise and set (Psalm 50:1), the rain and snow to fall (Job 37:6-13), directs the decisions of even seemingly random events (Proverbs 16:33), and watches over nations (Psalm 22:28, Acts 14:16, 17:26).

On a personal level, He has ordained all of the days of your life before you were ever born (Psalm 139:16). He fashions your heart (Psalm 33:14-15) and orders your steps (Psalm 37:23, Proverbs 16:9, 20:24). It is your faith, or your trust in God, that is being tested. The testing does not produce the faith, but rather the trial reveals the faith you have. James tells you to turn your hardships into times of learning because tough times can teach you patience.

Patience is the Greek word *hupomone* and it comes from two words *hupo* (under) and *meno* (to stay, abide, remain). The word does not describe passive waiting but an active endurance. At its root, it literally means to remain under, stand fast and persevere as if one is under a heavy load and decisively remains there instead of trying to escape. Patience has its perfect work when faith chooses to remain through the hardship. God allows hardship and uses it to reveal His character, love and power. During life's trials, those who cling to our heavenly Father will find Him faithful and when the next trial arises, they will remember His faithfulness and to rest in Him, with joy, knowing that the testing of their faith produces patience. When we choose to endure trials by faith, with joy, it works to transform us into the image of

Christ and brings glory to our Lord and Savior. Choose joy in the testing of your faith and allow its perfect work to be revealed in you.

If we desire our faith to be strengthened we should not shrink from opportunities where our faith may be tried, and therefore, through trial, be strengthened.
~ George Mueller

Day 11

Faith Filled Expectations

Now faith is the substance of things hoped
for, the evidence of things not seen.
~ Hebrews 11:1

Do you remember how you felt as a child
when your birthday approached? You were
excited and anxious, looking forward to what
the day would bring. Perhaps it was the gifts,
a special trip, your favorite dinner, or a
birthday party being thrown in honor of your
day. No doubt you were filled with
expectations of what wonders awaited you.
Birthdays provided assurance and
anticipation and so does faith. Faith makes
things hoped for, as real as if they have
already happened. It brings the future within
the present and makes the invisible seen.

Matthew Henry said, "Faith and hope go
together; and the same things that are the
object of our hope are the object of our
faith."[6] Faith is confidence in the
dependability of God and the conviction to
believe based on past experience that what
God says is true and His promises will come
to pass. Yet too often we doubt, even in the
midst of God's faithfulness to us. Like
Thomas, our faith is anchored in our sight.
When told by the other disciples that the
resurrected Christ was present, Thomas
insisted he would not believe so until his own
fingers could touch the holes in Jesus' hands

and his own hand could reach into Christ's side (John 20:24-25).

Eight days later when Jesus appeared a second time to the disciples, this time with Thomas present, Christ simply invited Thomas to see and touch for himself so he could believe. Hearing the Savior's invitation was enough to move Thomas from doubt to worship and declare, "My Lord and my God!" (John 20:28). As believers we all occasionally experience times when we doubt and our lack of faith needs eyes to see or our fingers to touch the truth. But living by faith requires we release our need for our human senses to provide the evidence for our hope.

Instead we are to rely wholly on God. God has a plan for our life and is constantly directing circumstances and maneuvering people so His purpose is achieved. We may not yet be able to see what God's future plan is for our circumstances but we can have confidence that God will be in that future plan. There is rest when we understand that God has a plan for our future, and it is meant for our good, and not for evil (Jeremiah 29:11-13). God is faithful to His plan, as He promises that we will not be cut off from it (Proverbs 23:18). When we believe that God will fulfill His promises even though we do not yet see them materializing, we demonstrate true faith, the substance of things hoped for but not yet seen.

True faith sees the invisible, believes the unbelievable, and receives the impossible.

Though you cannot yet see all the birthday surprises, you can trust they will come to be. Though you may not yet see the results of your faith, you can trust that God will bring your faith filled expectations into some kind of possession, whether it be visible to your eyes or known to your soul, today or on some day in your future.

Faith, mighty faith, the promise sees,
and looks to God alone,
laughs at impossibilities,
and cries it shall be done.
~ Charles Wesley

Day 12

Watching and Waiting

For the vision is yet for an appointed time;
But at the end it will speak, and it will not
lie. Though it tarries, wait for it: Because it
will surely come, It will not tarry.
~ Habakkuk 2:3

How long? And why? Two questions the believer cries out when their circumstances are filled with destruction or the events around them seem out of control. Called from a priesthood to be God's prophet, Habakkuk found himself in such circumstances. Judah was in moral and spiritual decay under the captivity of Babylon. Gluttony, drunkenness, greed, pride, corruption, and idolatry filled the land. King Nebuchadnezzar had a lust for magnificence and conquest and spared no lives as slave labor built his dynasty. But God gave the prophet both a vision and hope as He reminds him, "I am aware of the days and have appointed a time when the destruction will end. Do not grow weary; wait, as I will not tarry one minute longer than needed."

What a beautiful promise for the believer to cling to when all seems lost and our heart is in despair. Whether it is ourselves or someone we love living in captivity and decay, God reassures us, He is present; He is sovereign over the circumstances and He has allowed this time for His good purpose (Philippians 2:13). He delivered Judah, and He will deliver each of us too. The key to peace amid the destruction is to keep our minds and hearts stayed on Him (Isaiah 26:3) because joy comes in the morning (Psalm 30:5). When we rely on God our faith can rest and rejoice in Him.

To rely on God fully means you trust His timing despite your understanding of the circumstances around you. Watching and waiting for a vision that tarries is the true test of our faithfulness to God. Choosing to worship God while we wait demonstrates our faithful obedience to His fulfillment of the vision rather than our own agenda. Our devotion to God is demonstrated by our commitment to remain within His will. God seldom performs His promises or answers our expectations till we are brought to this state of mind.

What circumstances have you doubting God's timing today? Have you asked God for something, and He asked you to wait? Have you run ahead of God, trying to help Him by bringing the vision to completion? Abraham and Sarah did this when they doubted God's promise to provide a son to them. They mistakenly helped to bring fulfillment to God's vision by birthing a son with Sarah's maidservant. Like Abraham and Sarah, we struggle to wait on God's timing because of our unbelief or impatience.

We must guard against impatience in judging the ways of God, and know how to wait. God has long waited upon us. He has had great patience with us, shall we not patiently wait for His appointed time to be brought to fulfillment? The sweetest of blessings is generally proportioned to the time we have waited for them (Psalm 103:2).

There are no 'ifs' in God's Kingdom. His timing is perfect. His will is our hiding place. Lord Jesus, keep me in Your will! Don't let me go mad by poking about outside it. ~ Corrie ten Boom

God's Purpose in You

*I know that You can do everything, And that
no purpose of Yours can be withheld
from You.* ~ Job 42:2

God sometimes uses loss and suffering for
His glorious purpose in our lives. Job's
suffering was not without purpose. It
revealed the character of God *to* Job, showing
a God who is deeply aware of our problems,
and a God who goes before us and who stands
with us as we endure. But Job's suffering also
revealed the character of God *in* Job. In this
same way our suffering is not without
purpose in our lives. How we handle
suffering will demonstrate the character of
God in us.

Questioning God's purpose in allowing loss
and pain in his life, Job requests an answer
from God (31:35). Though God's answer did
not vindicate Job (38:1-41:34), he does not
cry out for justice but instead confesses to
God that he has spoken about things he
knows nothing about (40:3-5). What an
amazing confession followed by his
proclamation in Job 42:2. Job realized he is
nothing in the presence of a holy God. Earlier
he had maintained his righteousness and
integrity (32:1), but having both seen and
heard the Lord, all he can now say is, "I
repent in dust and ashes" (42:6).

Even though Job had questions, even though he wrestled with doubt, once the Lord reminded Job of His purpose for all of creation, Job acknowledged that God can achieve all His plans, and that His plans are sovereign because He can do all things (Matthew 19:26). He is the author and finisher of our faith (Hebrews 12:2) and He knows the beginning from the end (Isaiah 46:10).

With his newly opened eyes of spiritual understanding, Job could accept God's way in his life – which at that point still included suffering. We may have questions. We may not know the answers. We may not understand why the Lord gives and takes away, but we, like Job, can proclaim, "I know that you can do everything, and that no purpose of Yours can be withheld from You." As you face a volatile world, and possibly an unpredictable or unjust situation, can you proclaim the same? In this same way, God instructed Job to leave justice, including his own vindication, in His hands (Job 40:7-14). How hard is that to do for you? To whom or what do you turn to provide vindication?

Even though the reason for our suffering may remain hidden in the midst of our circumstances, God allows it for a divine purpose. We can trust that His ways are better than our own (Isaiah 55:8-9). There is no circumstance in our lives that is without His purpose to complete the work He began in each of us (Philippians 1:6). Like Job, sometimes it is only our perspective that hinders God's work from being done. Are you so caught up in your own pain and suffering that you cannot see or hear the purpose in God's amazing plan for you? Take heed of our friend Job and repent! "Commit your way to the LORD, trust also in Him, and He shall bring it to pass" (Psalm 37:5).

Faith is deliberate confidence in the character of God whose ways you may not understand at the time. ~ Oswald Chambers

Faithful Fire

He will sit as a refiner and a purifier of
silver; He will purify ... and purge them as
gold and silver, that they may offer to the
Lord an offering of righteousness.
~ Malachi 3:3

The refining process in the Old Testament days was time-consuming and laborious work. The unyielding ore had to first be mined, then pounded, shattered and crushed into a fine powder by primitive hand tools. The remaining powder, comprised of the precious metal (gold or silver), rock minerals and dirt along with other unwanted materials, was then washed to remove some of the unwanted material until only the metallic elements were left behind. Placing the metal in a crucible (melting pot), the refiner then heated the metal to high temperatures.

As the metal heated, the dross (impurities) separated from the liquid and rose to the top where it was skimmed off by the refiner. This heating process was repeated as many times as was necessary in order to increase the quality and purity of the metal, until all that was left was pure silver or pure gold. The refiner knew the process was done, when leaning forward to look in the crucible, he could see his own image reflected in the metal. When the refiner saw his own reflection he knew the metal was ready to take a new and perfect shape in the mold. It was only this refined (purified) metal that was used in the building of God's Tabernacle and His Temple.

God knows the value of the refiner's fire as He seeks to perfect holiness in His children. His work in our lives is much like the refiner's purifying fire perfecting its work in each of us, first by removing us from the hard rock of sin, then washing us in baptism and allowing the heat of our circumstances to purify us (Zechariah 13:9), with each trial making us more into the image of His own Son.

God alone sits as the refiner. Pastor F. B. Meyer says, "What a comfort it is that He surrenders this work to no other hands than his own. He may give his angels charge concerning us when we are in danger; but he keeps our purification beneath his special superintendence. "[7] Like a good refiner God sits close, He never leaves the crucible, watching the work carefully and constantly, never allowing the fire to destroy us completely. As we are purified by God, His reflection in us becomes more and more evident to those around us.

If you are now in the fire, be encouraged, it shows that you are precious metal, and God desires to prepare you for another work to prove the genuineness of your faith as the heat reveals the sin and corruption to be lifted out (1 Peter 1:6-7). Allow the heat, discomfort and adversity to draw you into a deeper intimacy with God. We may not understand why God is allowing particular circumstances but we can, like Job, declare that God alone "knows the way I take; when he has tested me, I will come forth as gold" (Job 23:10). What is God using to refine you? What impurities do you think these trials can remove from your heart?

A gem cannot be polished without friction,
nor a man perfected without trials.
~ Lucius Annaeus Seneca

Day 15

Consider the Lilies

*Consider the lilies, how they grow: they
neither toil nor spin; and yet I say to you,
even Solomon in all his glory was not
arrayed like one of these.* ~ Luke 12:27

Man adds nothing to the perfection of God's
creation. The lilies of the field are God's
workmanship and each one serves its purpose
in creation. They neither toil nor spin, nor
labor to the point of exhaustion. The flowers,
as they bloom, are beautiful, content and
glad. With no effort other than their
obedience to respond to God as they were
designed to do, they are more glorious than
Solomon clothed in all his fine riches
enthroned among the works of his own
hands.

We can learn from the lilies. The same God
who provides for the lilies will provide for us
as well, once we release our resolve on doing
it ourselves. This does not mean we will not
have to labor, but it does mean if we are
surrendered and focused on obeying God's
design and plan for us, our needs will be met.
Nothing we do in our efforts could ever be as
beautiful as God's work in us. He is able to
supply all our needs (Philippians 4:19) and do
so exceedingly, abundantly more than we
could even think to ask for (Ephesians 3:20-
21). There is nothing more beautiful to God
than His creation obeying His purpose.

To *consider* literally means "to think from up to down" and come to a conclusion. The implication is that careful attention be given so that a full and clear understanding will come. It is the same consideration Moses gave to the burning bush (Exodus 3:2), the same consideration we are to give to the faithfulness of Christ (Hebrews 3:1-2), and the same consideration we are commanded to in being doers of the word and not just hearers (James 1:22).

Pastor Dietrich Bonhoeffer, an influential theologian who was martyred under the Nazi regime, said, "For faith is only real when there is obedience, never without it, and faith only becomes faith in the act of obedience."[8] In order to have faith, some sort of action [obedience] must be initiated. You do not know whether water will flow from the spigot until you turn the handle on. You do not know if a kite will fly until you release it to the power of the wind. And you will not realize the amazing power of God's love until you turn your life over to Him and release your soul to His purpose and plan for you. You demonstrate your faith by obeying His commands and trusting His Word.

As Christians, we must allow God's Word to shape our character until the natural outcome is obedience. We must be willing, like the lilies, to submit our lives to His purpose and plan for each of us. This is what it means to grow. When we do so, under the protection and power of God's love, we will serve God's purpose for us in His creation. When we serve our purpose in obedience, by the strength that He supplies, then God will be glorified (1 Peter 4:11). We receive this supply by faith. It is a moment by moment trust that what we need will be supplied: life, breath, and everything. The Lord cares for His creation and He cares for you. Oh, that we, like the lilies, could mirror back to heaven God's glory as it shines in us!

Faith is the bird that sings when the dawn is still dark. ~ Scandinavian Saying

Do Not Worry,
Be Anxious for Nothing

If then God so clothes the grass, which today is in the field and tomorrow is thrown into the oven, how much more will He clothe you, O you of little faith? ~ Luke 12:28

In the midst of His loving correction to the disciples about worry, Jesus asks in Luke 12:26, "If then you are not able to do the least, why are you anxious for the rest?" The question was meant to direct the disciples' attention from their worry over food, clothing, and the length of one's life on to more eternal matters. It would have been a radical and outrageous statement for Jesus to tell His listeners, living in lack and limitation, that there was no need to worry or to be anxious over life's daily concerns.

Worry and anxiety are completely counter-productive and are rooted in disobedience. Worry happens when we assume responsibility God never intended us to have. Our assumptions then cause us to run and chase self-fulfilling prophecies or keep us stuck, immovable, filled with fear of unknown outcomes. Anxiety is a distraction that draws us in the opposite direction of faith. The word literally means to be pulled apart or divided into parts. Both worry and anxiety produce stress in our life that does nothing but destroy our faith in God.

To be "of little faith" (*oligópistos*) describes someone who lacks confidence in Christ. Are you dull to hearing the Lord's voice or disinterested in walking intimately with Him? This is literally what it means to be of little faith! We prove ourselves "of little faith" when we are anxious and worry and rush around in a senseless struggle to get more. We waste our lives doing what God has already promised to do for us, if we had only obediently devoted our time and talents to Him.

Worry and anxiety do not disappear because we close our eyes to them, but because we know a loving God is greater than all our needs. Trusting in God is both reasonable and wise, as the evidence is all around us. Look at how He cares for the birds who have no storehouses for food, the flowers who depend on the rain and the sun only He can provide, or even the grass that withers, which is not yet done, as it provides kindling for the oven.

Paul gave the church of Philippi some excellent advice about worry and anxiety when he wrote, "Be anxious for nothing, but in everything by prayer and supplication, with thanksgiving, let your requests be made known to God; and the peace of God, which surpasses all understanding, will guard your hearts and minds through Christ Jesus (Philippians 4:6-7). Paul's advice is to turn your worries into prayers. As you pray, remember, God has given you His promises, His protection, and His provision. You have a choice. You can keep worrying, and ruin your mental and physical health, and hinder your spiritual growth. Or you can cast your cares on the strong shoulders of your loving Savior who has promised to give you His peace.

Worrying is carrying tomorrow's load with today's strength – carrying two days at once. It is moving into tomorrow ahead of time. Worrying doesn't empty tomorrow of its sorrow, it empties today of its strength.
~ Corrie ten Boom

Faith in His Work

. . . being confident of this very thing, that
He who has begun a good work in you will
complete it until the day of Jesus Christ. ~
Philippians 1:6

God's work *for us* began when Christ died on the cross in our place. His work *in us* began when we first believed and were saved to eternal life. As a child of God, every aspect of our life – mind, attitudes and behaviors – are to be transformed by the Holy Spirit's good work in us, enabling us to be more like Christ every day. This is the process of Christian growth and maturity that began at salvation and will continue until Christ returns again.

Yet, like any growing child, we will stumble and fall. When we do, discouragement often comes to visit. One of Satan's favorite devices is discouragement. When he cannot keep us from getting saved, he will do his best to discourage us from growing by reminding us of past failures, current weaknesses, or stealing our confidence in the future. When this happens, our eyes are on ourselves rather than the Lord. We neglect God's work in us and when we remove our eyes from Him, the Author and Finisher of our faith (Hebrews 12:2), we mistakenly try to complete work He began and has promised to finish in us.

The Greek word for *complete* means that God will carry it through to perfection; He will not leave it unfinished; He will not begin the work and then abandon it. Paul was confident of this promise and used strong language in saying so. *Being confident* literally means to be fully and firmly persuaded or convinced. Paul was entirely convinced of the truth of what he said. It is the language of a man who had no doubt on the subject. Why did Paul have such confidence, particularly since he was writing this letter to the church from prison?

The original language implies Paul's confidence involved obedience that was the result of God's persuasion. This persuasion began on the road to Damascus and continued through Paul's missionary journeys. Yet Paul's obedience to the gospel had landed him in prison. But even this only served to persuade him more and build his confident assurance of the love, power and faithfulness of God. Paul chose to joyfully focus on these truths as he wrote from prison. His consistent habit of prayer and living in and by the Spirit of God proved his confidence in God, gave him joy in the midst of his circumstances and reassured him that God was working to complete the spiritual growth He had begun in him.

Do you sometimes feel like you are not making any progress in your spiritual growth? When you feel incomplete, unfinished, discouraged or distressed by your shortcomings and weaknesses, remember God's promise and provision to complete the work He began in you. Do not let your present circumstances rob you of the joy of knowing Christ or keep you from growing closer to Him.

Faith is not knowing what the future holds, but knowing who holds the future.

Day 18

Non-Negotiable Faith

*For all the promises of God in Him are Yes,
and in Him Amen, to the glory of God
through us.* ~ 2 Corinthians 1:20

More than seven thousand of God's promises are recorded in the Bible. When He makes a promise, He keeps it. He cannot lie, so therefore, what the Father says He will do, He always accomplishes. The church in Corinth had been taught this, but false teachers were corrupting the teachings of the apostles concerning Christ. Paul was seeking to turn their attention from the charges made against him back to Jesus, or in other words, to the faithful One whom he had preached to them.

Today is no different with its own false teachers and leaders. When we hear the word *promise* it is often met with skepticism or disbelief. The world's broken promises keep heaping up and we doubt God's provision and concern for us. Many people say they believe God is who He says He is, that He is able to do what He says He will do, but they hesitate to believe God is willing to work in their lives. But God answers, "Since all my promises about my Son are true, you can trust the promises I give to you; Yes, you can trust them too!"

When you do not believe God is willing to keep His promises, you are not walking in faith. Rather than believe, you ask God if He actually promised something. Or you question His timing, particularly when the waiting gets long. While asking God for confirmation of His promises is not wrong, the time spent in doubt could be better spent developing an awareness of His presence, remaining steadfast in the infallible truth of His Word, and learning to trust God with the outcome.

To develop an awareness of God's presence, we must spend time in prayer. It is in prayer that we learn to discern God's voice. This helps us to understand that God's promises are for all of His children. He never withholds anything from us without a specific purpose – some of which we will never know. Trusting God with the outcome requires obedience that transcends our understanding but brings confidence that we serve a powerful God.

Shadrach, Meshach and Abednego were men who trusted God with the outcome. Depending on God to deliver them however He chose to, they made an unwavering and non-negotiable decision to not serve other gods and were thrown into a fiery furnace as a result (Daniel 3). Though they had to first walk into the fire, God showed up in the fire!

In the same way, you may go through fiery trials and the outcome of those troubles may look nothing like you hoped. When you make an unwavering decision to trust God no matter what may come – no matter how long the wait, God will always deliver you out of the hand of the enemy and into His promise, because He who calls you is faithful and keeps His promises (1 Thessalonians 5:4, 2 Timothy 2:13).

God never made a promise that was too good to be true. ~ Dwight L. Moody

Resist Not, But Abound

*We are bound to thank God always for you,
brethren, as it is fitting, because your faith
grows exceedingly, and the love of every one
of you all abounds toward each other.*
~ 2 Thessalonians 1:3

The crux of Christian life is faith and love.
Faith is the vertical response to God's grace
and confidence in His care for us. Love is the
horizontal response to grace in carrying out
the command to love others as exampled by
Jesus. Faith and love, together, separate us in
to holiness. Challenged by affliction, the faith
of the church in Thessalonica remained
firmly rooted in Christ, as evidenced by their
love toward one another, though they were no
longer patient in hope for Christ's return (1
Thessalonians 1:3).

We find both rejoicing and a rebuke as we
look at the beauty of their growth. On one
hand, it is a comfort to know both our faith
and love will continue to grow, that none of
us has arrived yet. This is contrary to how we
often speak of faith. Anglican preacher John
Stott makes a good observation of this when
he says, "We tend to speak of faith in static
terms as something we either have or have
not. 'I wish I had your faith', we say, like 'I
wish I had your complexion', as if it were a
genetic endowment. Or we complain 'I've
lost my faith' like 'I've lost my spectacles',

as if it were a commodity. ... It is similar with love. We assume rather helplessly that we either love somebody or we do not, and that we can do nothing about it. But love also, like faith, is a living relationship, whose growth we can take steps to nurture."[9] Through the work of the Holy Spirit both faith and love grow in us as our faith and love for God grow.

The rebuke comes by way of all the missed opportunities for growth in faith and love we did not pursue or we resisted. Missed opportunities grieve the Holy Spirit (Ephesians 4:30), quench His fire inside of us (1 Thessalonians 5:19), and hinder our own spiritual growth (Acts 7:51). How or when do we miss opportunities? When we do not read God's Word, the Holy Spirit cannot illuminate the truth to us. When God's Word is not being illuminated in to our lives, there is no intimacy with God. When there is no intimacy with God, we are not moving toward Christlikeness. When we are not moving toward Christlikeness, there is no glory for Christ. When there is no glory for Christ, it is because we either serve His Kingdom for self-fulfilling reasons or we do not serve at all.

The work of the Holy Spirit is to move you along a path of ever increasing faith and love because it leads to holiness. He wants to make you holy. What does holy mean? To be separate, set apart. He wants to separate you further and further from sin. As you get further and further from sin, the closer you grow to God. Three things happen as you grow closer to God. First, the power of temptation and desires to fulfill the flesh diminish. Second, your preoccupation with the world fades. And third, your longing for God intensifies. As you move toward God you grow in faith and thereby abound in love, the greatest command, and become more like Jesus each day. Resist not the work of the Holy Spirit, choose to abound in His grace!

The true, living faith which the Holy Spirit instills into the heart, simply cannot be idle.
~ Martin Luther

Day 20

The Outworking of Faith

*For assuredly, I say to you, whoever says to
this mountain, 'Be removed and be cast into
the sea,' and does not doubt in his heart, but
believes that those things he says will be
done, he will have whatever he says.*
~ Mark 11:23

Faith unspoken is not faith at all. Like the fig
tree cursed by Jesus, we may look faithful
from a distance, but after closer examination,
if there is no fruit, we are spiritually barren
(Mark 11:12-14). Religious profession
without spiritual reality is an abomination to
God and is cursed. Just as the visible signs of
figs on the tree demonstrated the tree's
fruitfulness, our faith must become visible to
others. It is not enough to hope quietly or pray
inwardly for the mountain to be moved. Jesus
told us to speak aloud to the mountain. Why?
For the same reason Paul told us to confess
with our mouth that Jesus is Lord (Romans
10:9-10) and the author of Hebrews reminds
us that when God gives a promise, we are to
boldly speak it (Hebrews 13:5-6). Our faith
must be in the One who is able to move
mountains, so that when we verbally
command, "Mountain be moved and cast into
the sea," it will be done.

Faith in God overcomes insurmountable
odds. Faith justifies us (Romans 5:1),
removing the mountains of guilt and casting

them into the depths of the sea (Micah 7:19). Faith purifies the heart (Acts 15:9) and removes the mountains of corruption, making them plains before the grace of God (Zechariah 4:7). When our fears of the approaching army are given over to faith, God scatters the mountains of worry and makes the hills bow down (Habakkuk 3:6).

God, can do anything, and He will answer prayer but not as a response to the power of positive thinking or the shallow or distant appearance of faith. He cannot answer our prayers if we hold unforgiveness against another (Mark 11:25), or if we pray for selfish reasons (James 4:3). Our faith and requests must be according to God's will for His Kingdom. Every act of faith must rest on God's promises and when they do, any mountain we command to be removed, will be cast into the sea.

What mountain looms in front of you? Do you doubt God's faithfulness with an unsaved loved one, a prodigal child, a lost job, an unexpected death, a serious illness, or a challenge in ministry? When you talk to God about them, do you ask according to His will? To pray effectively, you need faith in God, not the faith in the object of your request. If you only focus on your request, you will be left with nothing if God refuses your request. When Jesus prayed in the Garden of Gethsemane, He expressed His desires. He knew and declared aloud that all things are possible with God, but He prayed with God's interest in mind, God's intentions over His own desires "… nevertheless, not what I will, but Your will be done" (Mark 14:36).

Align your prayers with God's will and then whatever your circumstances, wherever the mountain, have faith in God, pray according to His will, and do not doubt that your faith will move mountains.

Your faith can move mountains and your doubt can create them!

Day 21

Faith Reaches Out

*But Jesus turned around, and when He saw
her He said, "Be of good cheer, daughter;
your faith has made you well." And the
woman was made well from that hour.*
~ Matthew 9:22

For twelve years she had been untouchable.
Like a leper or the demon-possessed she was
considered unclean. Levitical law forbid her
from socializing or touching anyone
considered clean, and separated her from God
because no atonement could be made for her
(Leviticus 15:25). But Jesus the Pure One (1
John 3:3) changed that and restored her. It
was the power of Jesus that cured her; but that
power would not have been exerted if not for
the woman's faith to press in and reach out
for just a touch from even the hem of the
Master's garment. True faith goes beyond the
curiosity of the crowd and reaches out and
touches Him.

Both Mark and Luke record that Jesus
inquired as to who had touched His garment.
Peter and the other disciples questioned why
He would focus on one particular touch when
the crowds pressed in around Him. His
response: He felt power go out from Him.
Jesus knew a healing had taken place. True
faith never goes unnoticed by God.

Scanning the crowd, the Messiah's eyes landed on her. Jesus saw her – in a crowd, pressing in and reaching out for just one healing touch from Him, His eyes fastened on the woman who had touched Him and received healing. Perceiving that she could not go undiscovered, she came trembling to Him, fell down before Him, and told Him the whole truth. Luke's account states she testified to her immediate healing in the presence of all the people. True faith cannot be practiced in isolation from others.

For twelve years, this woman had been separated from family, friends and God. Medical science had let her down as she spent her livelihood looking for a cure to what afflicted her. How easily it might have been for her to give up. Sometimes we give up on people or circumstances that have not changed. Sometimes we feel our problems will keep us from God. But He is always ready to help. God can change what seems unchangeable, giving new purpose and new hope. We should never allow our fear to keep us from approaching Him and the power of His touch. Our faith must be greater than our fear because true faith releases God's power to make us well.

Many people are vaguely familiar with Jesus, but nothing in their lives has changed or bettered by His passing acquaintance. Are you just curious about God, or do you reach out to Him in faith, knowing that His mercy will bring healing to your body, soul and spirit? God heals – He is the great physician and He can heal anyone of any affliction, whether it be spiritual, physical, mental, emotional, or financial. There are going to be times in your life when you need God's touch. Do not be afraid to reach out for His healing touch. Be faith-filled, make plans and move on in spite of what afflicts you. Then when God touches your life, do not be afraid to share the amazing details with family, friends and strangers.

Faith obliterates time, annihilates distance, and brings future things at once into its possession. ~ C. H. Spurgeon

Teachable Faith

*Immediately the father of the child cried out
and said with tears, "Lord I believe;
help my unbelief!"* ~ Mark 9:24

In a heart-rending cry of desperation, the father of a demon possessed child questions whether Jesus can do something to heal his son. Jesus replies, "You want me to do something? Let me ask you this one thing. Can you believe?" It is not a question of His ability to heal, but of the father's ability to believe. The father expressed the paradox of faith and unbelief that we all experience. We want to believe, but often, focused on what appears to be overwhelming circumstances, we find ourselves filled with doubt. It is an inward battle, and though we know it is an unreasonable contradiction, our fight seems futile.

We are not alone in our doubt. Throughout the pages of the Bible people questioned or doubted God – Adam, Sarah, Jacob, Job, Jeremiah, Habakkuk, Jonah, Thomas, Martha, and Peter. And there were some who should have known better – Jesus' own family and townspeople doubted Him. John the Baptist, his cousin questioned Him. Among those closest to Him, the 12 disciples, Thomas doubted Him, Peter cursed Him, Judas betrayed Him, and all abandoned Him in His darkest hours. But as with them, God can use our unbelief as a teachable moment.

It is in these moments that God reveals the root of our unbelief as a lack of faith in His sufficiency and control in our lives. Unbelief in God's ability to complete His work reveals our lingering reliance on our own strengths, our own abilities to reason through to a self-fulfilling outcome, or a kind of unnecessary suffering we put ourselves through when we refuse to give in to God entirely and take what He says with complete trust. But God can use our unbelief to remove the seeds of doubt and heighten our awareness of our need for total dependence on Him.

Moses learned to depend on God as he led the children of Israel out of Egypt (Exodus 3:10-15). Gideon experienced victory over doubt when God reduced his army to 300 men (Judges 7:2). Mute Zacharias praised God with his first words after months of silence due to doubt (Luke 1:64). The disciples witnessed Jesus calm both the storms of the sea and the troubles of their hearts (Matthew 8:26). And you, too, can depend on God to use your unbelief to deliver you to calmer seas.

Like the father of the demon possessed boy, you only need to ask God for His help. He is waiting to help you let go of your desires and surrender them to Him. To deal with your doubts, make sure your heart is submitted to God. Then, and only then, can Jesus give you aid as you pray, "Lord I believe; please help me with my unbelief!" God is faithful to take your unbelief and turn your doubt into trust. Nothing is too difficult for Him. "If you can believe, all things are possible to him who believes" (Mark 9:23).

Oh, it is wonderful to know that our
Heavenly Father loves us, - even with all
our flaws! His love is such that even should
we give up on ourselves, He never will.
~ Joseph B. Wirthlin

Active Faith

Then Jesus said to him, "Go your way; your faith has made you well." And immediately he received his sight and followed Jesus on the road. ~ Mark 10:52

Bartimaeus knew who Jesus was and had heard of his fame for healing, but until now he had no means of making contact with the Son of David, a clear reference and title for the Messiah (Mark 10:47). Determined to get near the one person who could meet his need, he cries out to Jesus, even in the face of opposition, until he gets the Savior's attention. This incident reveals something important about how God interacts with us. Jesus is willing to act on our persistent requests and because Bartimaeus had eyes of faith and believed, Jesus healed his physical sight. Bartimaeus' response? He immediately followed Jesus.

The incident also reveals something important about how we respond to God's grace and mercy. Those with the spiritual eyesight to see Christ, will draw near to Him to run after Him. Active faith follows Jesus. Bartimaeus went from sitting on the roadside, hidden in a crowd determined to keep him both blind and invisible, to casting aside every hindrance to follow Jesus on the road to Jerusalem.

His only possession, a beggar's cloak used to collect hand-outs, was thrown aside so that it would not get in his way as he approached Jesus. By casting it aside, Bartimaeus was forsaking his former way of life, completely confident that Jesus would heal him and provide for all his needs. In contrast to the rich man (Mark 10:17-22), Bartimaeus left everything he had and followed Jesus. He is the picture of true discipleship – he recognized his own need for a Savior, calls out to Jesus, leaves all behind to receive what Christ can offer and then follows Him in response to his healing.

We, too, can be like a beggar sitting on the roadside, receiving the world's crumbs, trying to catch glimpses of God's glory, hoping for all our needs to be met. Or we can be like Bartimaeus, willing to get rid of anything that comes between us and Jesus. Can you say you are ready to throw off every hindrance? What keeps you from surrendering all you have to Jesus Christ? Jesus asked Bartimaeus, "What do you want me to do for you?" If Jesus asks you the same question, what will be your answer? What do you want Jesus to do in your life? Are you willing to set aside anything that hinders you and come to Him and put your trust in Him?

Paul tells us our unveiled faces provide all the sight we need to be transformed daily (2 Corinthians 3:18). The writer of Hebrews encourages us by reminding us who is in the stands, rooting for us, as we throw off everything that hinders and the sin that so easily entangles to run with perseverance the road already marked out for us (Hebrews 12:1-2). We must be willing to give up whatever compromises our relationship with God. We should be running toward Christ and we should always keep Him in our sight. Do not wait – commit now to follow Jesus more closely as you seek to become more like Him.

All I have seen teaches me to trust the Creator for all I have not seen.
~ Ralph Waldo Emerson

Faith Stands Together

Above all, taking the shield of faith with
which you will be able to quench all the
fiery darts of the wicked one.
~ Ephesians 6:16

The shield to which Paul referred was a large, oblong Roman shield which looked like a full door. To get to the soldier, the enemy had to get past the *door*. The shield was used to quench flame tipped arrows launched at the soldier either from the ground or the air. A large metal knob in the center, called a boss, was used to defensively push an attacker back, throwing the enemy off balance. Paul says that we must take up this shield, literally raise it. It is not something that happens automatically because we are a believer. Rather, we must actively trust in God when the enemy's arrows fly or he is advancing on us.

While a physical shield protects us physically, it is faith that protects us spiritually even in the midst of our physical trials and circumstances. Our trust must rest in God our shield (Psalm 7:10) and Jesus our door (John 10:9). It is God alone who breaks the arrows of our enemies (Psalm 76:3) and Jesus who delivers us from the hands of our enemy (Luke 1:71). Our faith in God, as demonstrated by Christ, can give Satan a good shove backwards and give us a chance to fight back while doing God's will and work.

The only time Satan's tactics can defeat us is when we drop our shield, when we compromise our faith, when we stop believing God is in control or that He is working everything out for our good. When we allow fear, doubt or worry to creep in, as Peter did when anxious about the waves, we will start to sink (Matthew 14:30). But when our faith in God's sovereign presence and care for us is strong, it is impossible for Satan to break through our shield and win an attack.

If you are saved, you are on the battleground. You are at war and faith is everything as you face the fiery darts of Satan. There may be times you want to surrender. But you can wage a winning war not just as a survivor, but as more than a conqueror (Romans 8:37) because God is your shield when you put your trust in Him (Psalm 18:30, Proverbs 30:5). Faith conquers Satan's cunning and crafty darts of temptation and attempts to isolate us (1 Peter 5:9). Faith overcomes the world (1 John 5:4) and thereby the prince of the world (1 John 5:18).

When the army moved ahead, the soldiers in the front row put their shields side by side, forming a wall of defense. Every row behind the first row would raise their shields overhead, thereby forming one large protective shield around the army. While each soldier had to raise his own shield, the strength came by doing it with all the others. So while each believer must take up the shield of faith individually, we do it together with others who are trusting God in the battle. You will be stronger in the battle when you know your brothers and sisters down the line are fending off the enemy's arrows with their shields. We must stand together and pray for one another, so that we can encourage one another in the fight of faith.

The most damaging, most powerful weapon is one tiny seed of faith.

Day 25

Little Things Are the Big Things

His lord said to him, "Well done, good and faithful servant; you have been faithful over a few things, I will make you ruler over many things. Enter into the joy of your lord." ~ Matthew 25:23

If we are faithful stewards of small things, then we will be faithful when God gives us more. The difference, as Jesus explained in this parable, is whether we are shackled to the cares of earth or Kingdom minded, storing our treasure in heaven. The lesson is that God gives us something of considerable value and expects good stewardship and a return on what He has given. The servants who used their talents to bring more to their master, were blessed and received God's favor. But the servant who buried his talent, made excuses for his actions and even accused the master of being unfair, was called lazy and wicked and lost his talent to the more faithful servant.

The talents represent the riches we receive from God. It may be money, time, gifts, skills or other resources. God has made us caretakers of what He has provided and entrusted them to us. We are to wisely and generously use these resources. We will all be called to account for what we have been given, not for how much we were given, but for what we did with the talents God provided. God expects us to invest wisely toward heaven's storehouses with these things until Jesus returns.

David was a young man faithful in little things. Already anointed as king, he continued in the little things – feeding the sheep, and delivering supplies to the army fighting the Philistines, while bringing word back to his father about his brothers' welfare (1 Samuel 17:13-18). His faithfulness to the little things continued to prepare him for the giant things to come and his future reign as king. In a similar way, our physical life serves as preparation, a training ground, for something far greater. Our life now is meant to prepare us for our part in the coming Kingdom of God. With this understanding, God expects us to act accordingly and live each day in obedience with that goal and purpose in mind.

We must guard against the lazy and wicked servant's attitude. His *cannot* was really *will not*. Fear of the unknown future prevented him from obeying his master. He had forgotten the master's providential care over each of his servants, forgotten the master provided according to each one's ability (v. 15). Like the servants in the parable, none of us receive more or less than we can handle. God knows exactly what to give each of us to prepare us for the future.

Are you doing all you can with what you have been given or are you guilty of burying your talents? With what do you need to be more faithful? Commit today to use your life and all the resources God has given you, for His purposes, as a period of preparation, a training ground, for the coming Kingdom of God. Remember – being obedient and faithful is a daily process. We must continually rely on Him and His strength to live our lives in faithful service.

Be faithful in the small things because it is in them that your strength lies.
~ Mother Theresa

Seed of Faith

So Jesus said to them, "Because of your unbelief; for assuredly, I say to you, if you have faith as a mustard seed, you will say to this mountain, 'Move from here to there,' and it will move; and nothing will be impossible for you." ~ Matthew 17:20

Even a little faith can change the landscape. Faith can part the sea (Exodus 14:21), raise the valleys and level the hills (Isaiah 40:4), collapse the walls man has built (Joshua 6:20) and cause the unseen, the impossible, the seemingly absurd things from the world's viewpoint to be changed when our faith is based on the commands or promises of God. "By faith Sarah herself also received strength to conceive seed, and she bore a child when she was past the age, because she judged Him faithful who had promised" (Hebrews 11:11). There is nothing that is too difficult for the Lord. Nothing is impossible when our faith is rooted in the fruit only God can provide.

Faith is demonstrated by action; it is obedience to do what God has commanded us to do. When God commanded, Moses had to first raise his staff and stretch out his hand, both Joshua and Isaiah had to open their mouths to see obstacles removed, and Abraham and Sarah had to follow God's leading to give birth to God's promise. But too often we become frustrated and defeated because our needs, wants, expectations, and demands are not met immediately when we believe. We become impatient and want to quit.

Are you discouraged because the attainment of your goal seems far away? Are you disheartened because you cannot yet see the fruit of your faith? Do you try to dictate solutions to God? Or are you truly surrendered to the answers He may have that are far beyond your ability to imagine? Be encouraged, Jesus guarantees a seed not yet planted and as tiny as the mustard seed can change your circumstances.

A seed is dead until it is planted. Then after it is planted, it cannot be seen until it receives nourishment, such as good soil, water and sunshine. In order to grow, the seed needs to be dropped in dirt, covered in darkness, and then with proper care, it labors to reach the light. But when it finally breaks through the soil, it is not immediately a mature tree. It must continue to receive proper care and nourishment. In the same way, belief planted in the soil of God's promises will grow from a dead seed to a great tree, capable of changing the landscape. God plants the seed of faith in our hearts, then with the proper care, water and sun, it grows to a sprout, then to a sapling until its taproot takes hold and the tree gets all the rooting and source of nourishment it needs to mature.

Every part of God's creation begins with a seed. He is able to change circumstances, but will use our circumstances to grow our faith from a tiny dead seed, unseen to human eye, until it sprouts and yields to the promise He has prepared from our circumstances. If we really believe, if we really have confidence in God's Word, then we will take action, we will pray, we will plant, and we will trust God for the increase because only God can water and nourish the growth of our faith into all it was meant to be.

Faith is permitting ourselves to be seized by the things we do not see. ~ Martin Luther

Day 27

Strength from the Vine

*I can do all things through Christ who
strengthens me.* ~ Philippians 4:13

Did Paul actually mean there was nothing he
could not do? Can we, as believers, literally
do all things? For Paul, the answer was a
resounding, "Yes!" However, the certainty of
Paul's declaration meant "all things which
were God's will for him to do." Paul had
learned that God's commands are His
enablement. For Paul, and for us, the strength
to do all things rests in obedience to walk in
God's will and rely upon the power of the
Holy Spirit we receive in union with Christ as
we do so.

To abide in Christ and His strength is
illustrated in John 15. Christ is the vine and
we are the branches (John 15:5). The branch,
itself cannot live without being attached to
the vine. It receives its life, its strength, and
subsequently its growth and fruit by allowing
the life of the vine to flow through the branch.
Paul had learned this reliance many times
over. He had been beaten, stoned, lashed,
shipwrecked, imprisoned, robbed, left naked
and hungry, and faced many perils along with
frequent sickness (2 Corinthians 11:22-33).
He dealt constantly with a thorn in his flesh
(2 Corinthians 12:7). But in all these things,
done for Christ's sake, his character was

built, his faith was demonstrated and he was prepared for further service to the Lord.

Paul knew God would never call on him to accomplish anything without giving him the necessary grace (2 Corinthians 12:9). Whenever we begin to believe we are the only one suffering from a particular thorn in the flesh, we need to recall that Jesus absorbed not a single thorn in His flesh, but a crown of thorns, pressed into His skull (Mark 15:17). He can relate to whatever challenge we face because He is the vine and God is the vinedresser, who provides the strength we need to endure. Paul prayed three times for his thorn to be removed and Jesus prayed three times in the Garden of Gethsemane for the cup to be taken, but both permitted God's will to remain in their circumstances to strengthen them to walk in God's will.

Like Paul, we do not need to ask God for His grace to be sufficient in us, because it already is. When we pray we should not ask, "Lord help me to live my life for you." Instead, it would be better to pray, "Lord live out Your life through me." The purpose of your prayers should not be to ask God to remove your thorns and trials. The purpose of your prayers should be to ask God to give you Himself, His power, so that you might endure and grow in faith through those circumstances. It is when you are close to God, that His strength is made known to you and you discover His sufficient grace.

God does not guarantee you superhuman ability to accomplish anything you can imagine without regard to His interests. As you walk in faith, you will face troubles, pressures, and trials. Abiding in Christ will bring grace sufficient to do God's will and to face the challenges that arise from your commitment to doing so. As your challenges come, ask Christ to strengthen you and then draw on the life offered to you through the vine.

With trials we grow stronger in faith, with
faith we move closer to God,
with God we can do all things.

Day 28

Journey to Jerusalem

*But they did not receive Him, because His
face was set for the journey to Jerusalem.*
~ Luke 9:53

The disciples had been sent ahead to prepare
the way for Jesus through a Samaritan village
on their journey toward Jerusalem. But the
Samaritan village rejected the disciples.
What was it in Jesus' countenance that
caused the Samaritan village to reject him
and his disciples? Luke tells us, the villagers
recognized His countenance was set for the
journey to Jerusalem. Having been rejected
by the Jewish people for centuries, the
Samaritans had grown to detest anything or
anyone Jewish.

Rather than retaliate, knowing man's frailties
and shortcomings, Jesus moves on. Despite
James' and John's angry desire to call down
fire upon the Samaritans, Jesus rebukes them
and set His face toward His destination –
Jerusalem. Jesus kept moving forward, in
spite of rejection, in spite of ridicule, in spite
of threats by religious leaders, and even in
spite of well-intentioned distractions from
His followers. The irony is that Jerusalem
was the place of the cross. But the Apostle
Mark tells us that Jesus led the way on this
journey, and the disciples were both amazed
and afraid (Mark 10:32).

Afraid – because they had heard Jesus tell them several times by now that he would be delivered up to the cross, and despite Jesus' specific details about his death this time, the disciples grew no closer to understanding His mission. Instead they argued and the sons of Zebedee asked Jesus about their position in heaven. But their fiery anger, play for power and position, and lack of understanding met more grace as Jesus uses this opportunity to instruct His followers about discipleship.

The disciples momentarily forgot that Jesus and His message brings life, not death. God has not privileged us with the opportunity of belief to use it to destroy people's lives but rather to be used as His vessel to bring salvation. But there is a cost to discipleship – a cost in the face of being mocked, ridiculed, and turned away as His disciple. The cost requires we lay aside our own agendas, desires and needs as we move forward, press in and set our hearts and minds on things above (Colossians 3:1-2).

Like Jesus, we will meet rejection, we will meet ridicule, and we will meet those who do not like us. And like Jesus, we have the same opportunity to keep our face set toward our destination. We must not look half-heartedly toward our Jerusalem [Heaven]. God is looking for disciples who will commit themselves to the journey and to His leadership. Jesus never deterred from the plan for which God sent Him. His face was set for the journey to Jerusalem in spite of all the opposition. His countenance was set to endure the cross for the joy that was set before Him (Hebrews 12:2). It is a willful act in the heart of the disciple to stay the course. Is your face set for the journey to Jerusalem? When other's look at your countenance, do they see Jesus in you?

What brings glory to God is not that we live without failure, but that we trust Him enough to get up and keep moving forward.

Promised Land

Watch, stand fast in the faith, be brave,
be strong. ~ 1 Corinthians 16:13

Watch for temptation (Mark 14:38), watch for the roaring lion (1 Peter 5:8), watch for false teachers (2 Timothy 4:5), and watch for the Lord's return (Matthew 24:42). Stand fast in the faith, as Jesus did, finishing the work God gave Him to do (John 17:4). Be brave, be constantly responsible and courageous in obedience as God reveals His will and you grow in the grace and knowledge of the Lord Jesus Christ (2 Peter 3:18). And be strong in the Lord and in the power of His might (Ephesians 6:10). Paul gave the Corinthian church their marching orders and we have ours too.

Three times Joshua was given a similar command from God, "be strong and courageous," as he set out to lead the nation of Israel into the promised land (Joshua 1:5-9). There were good reasons for Joshua to be brave and strong – he had God's promise in a sure victory (vv. 5-6), he had a safe guide in God's Word (vv. 7-8), and he had the sustaining power of God's presence with him (v. 9). We too have these promises as we persevere through hardships as more then conquerors (Romans 8:37) and allow the Holy Spirit to comfort us, teach us truth and guide us (John 16:8-13).

Certainly Joshua's new job of leading two million people into a strange, new land and conquering it was a challenge. But, God was with Joshua and He is with us as we face new challenges. We may not have to conquer nations, but every day we face tough circumstances, thorny people, and the temptation to give up or give in. However, God has promised He will never leave us or forsake us (Deuteronomy 31:6).

As Joshua received God's direction and these promises, he and the Israelites were camped on the east banks of the Jordan, at the very edge of the Promised Land. To receive the promise would mean they would have to "arise and cross over the Jordan" (Joshua 1:2). At a crossroads, they were faced with the opportunity to either enter into all God had planned for them, or to turn back and remain in their old lives. Jesus has asked those who would follow Him to do the same.

The Gospels record people dropping their nets, abandoning their wealth, leaving their homes and their families, giving up their prejudices and political ideologies, and laying aside their own hopes and expectations for the future. The Apostle Paul gave up everything to follow Christ and know His resurrection power (Philippians 3:10). Paul's goal was to know Christ, to be like Christ, and to be all God had planned him to be.

You have the same opportunity to know Christ and the power of His resurrection but it will require you to cross over your Jordans. What are you willing to give up or leave behind in order to receive all God has promised? What new promised land is God calling you to enter and conquer? By asking God to direct your path you, too, can conquer your challenges on the way to the promised land.

We ought to live every day as though we've come out of another world – but with the power of that world still upon us. We should live and speak and move in that power, and have our whole being in Jesus Christ.
~ John Wesley

Cross the Finish Line

*Therefore, since we are surrounded by such
a great cloud of witnesses, let us throw off
everything that hinders and the sin that so
easily entangles. And let us run with
perseverance the race marked out for us,
fixing our eyes on Jesus, the pioneer and
perfecter of faith. For the joy set before him
he endured the cross, scorning its shame,
and sat down at the right hand of the throne
of God.* ~ Hebrews 12:1-2 (NIV)

The race of faith is a marathon, not a series of
sprints. The Christian life involves hard work
and dedication toward a single goal, a finish
line we cannot yet see – Heaven. If we are to
run the race well, it will require us to forsake
anything that compromises our relationship
with God. We must run steadily and
patiently, and overcome sin through the
power of Holy Spirit. There will be sacrifice;
in fact, it will cost us everything (Luke 14:28-
33). But our focus is not on the hardship; it is
on Jesus, the author and perfecter of our faith,
and the One who will complete it (Philippians
1:6).

Our race has been set, the course marked out
for us. If we lose sight of it, we will stumble
as we look away from Jesus to look at
ourselves or life's circumstances. But if we
remember God's Word, our paths will be
filled with God's faithfulness (Psalm 25:10).

Our legs will tire from the duration of the race, but we must remember that suffering is the training ground for Christian maturity. It develops patience and makes our final victory sweet (James 1:2). The encouragement to keep running comes as we look to the grandstands, to the faithful ancestors who sit cheering us on, along with Jesus.

We must lay aside everything that hinders our journey toward heaven. The Apostle Paul said, we are to forget those things which are behind and reach forward to those things which are ahead, pressing toward the goal for the prize of the upward call (Philippians 3:12-14). This goal absorbed all of Paul's energy and it should absorb all of ours too. With the single-minded goal of an athlete in training, we must lay aside, cast aside, run from and forsake anything that distracts us from being effective in the Kingdom of God.

Are you weary from the race? Grumbling because the course God has set before you is harder than you imagined? Have you begun the race, only to take your eyes off Jesus and put them back on the trials and temptations that weigh you down and pull you back? Are you allowing life's circumstances to encumber your run toward the finish line? Your victor's crown awaits; will you forfeit it? Remember this: the end of your race, win or lose, is closer today than it was yesterday.

The crown of righteousness is promised to all who finish the course (2 Timothy 4:7-8). Jesus finished the race triumphantly. Those who belong to Him will do so also when He returns to gather his followers home and set them at His banquet table (Revelation 19:9). Get in the race, remember the course is marked, angels are cheering, eternity draws ever nearer. The joy of knowing and obeying Jesus is greater than all of the hardships and sufferings we might have to bear for His sake.

Faith is taking the first step even when you can't see the whole staircase.
~ Martin Luther King, Jr.

Thy Kingdom Come

And the Spirit and the bride say, "Come!"
And let him who hears say, "Come!" And let
him who thirsts come. Whoever desires, let
him take the water of life freely.
~ Revelation 22:17

It is an invitation of just one word. Jesus proclaimed it throughout His ministry to all He encountered. *Come* to me, *come* follow me, *come* as you are, *come* and see, *come* to the water. To Peter, who asked to walk on the water, Jesus simply said, "Come!" The invitation to come is given to a doomed and damned world that is lost and dying. It is an invitation to the Church to be ready for Christ's return.

But it is also a command to be met with immediate obedience when we hear God's voice. We must be like Peter, who, believing the command came with the strength to experience an unusual demonstration of God's power, jumped from the boat and found he could walk on the water (Matthew 14:29).

Let him who hears, come. The implication of the original language is that everyone who has ears should pay attention to the instruction that follows. We are offered a clear choice. Like Peter, we must have the faith to move when God speaks. Whether it is the day of our salvation or a single moment in our sanctification, when God says, "Come," we must respond without fear or doubt, ready to step out in faith to obey God, to demonstrate a living faith. Living faith moves when Jesus says, "Come!"

The Sea of Galilee was a place familiar to Peter. It is the location where Jesus first called Peter and his brother Andrew to be His disciples (Matthew 4:18-20). It is also the place where Jesus forgave Peter after he denied Him three times (John 21:1-19). Jesus is with us in the significant places where our faith is grown. When He says, "Come, follow me," He does not abandon us. He is there when we face trials. In the midst of the waves and the wind, He saves us from sinking.

We do not know what any of the other disciples were thinking as Peter jumped from the boat. It is possible some believed he was crazy, some may have murmured how quickly he would fail, and others how unpredictable his behavior was in following Christ. The world is quick to point out our failures, shortcomings and inconsistencies as we follow Christ too. Why? Because the world is determined to keep us out of the Kingdom of God.

Ultimately the consequences of our choices can be a matter of life or death. We will either say to Jesus, "Lord, Thy will be done," and accept the offer of eternal life with God, growing in likeness to Jesus until we are taken home to Heaven; or God will say to us, "Mankind, thy will be done" and then He will send us to a place where we will never have to hear His voice again.

Walking on water has nothing to do with water. It has everything to do with faith and faith has everything to do with hearing God's voice. ~ Rex Rouis

Endnotes:

[1] Corrie Ten Boon, *The Hiding Place*, (Bloomington, MN: Chosen Books, 1984).

[2] Charles H. Spurgeon, *Spurgeon's Sermons*, Volume 17, Sermon No. 979, "Faith and Regeneration," March 5, 1871.

[3] C. H. Mackintosh, *Genesis to Deuteronomy: Notes on the Pentateuch*. 6 vols. (New York: Loizeaus Brothers, 1879).

[4] Max Lucado, *The Gift for All People: Thoughts on God's Great Grace*, (Sisters, OR: Multnomah, 1999).

[5] John Calvin, the first extant writing to contain the phrase is John Calvin's *Antidote to the Council of Trent* (1547). For context, Calvin was responding to Canon 11 of the sixth session of the Council of Trent: "Whosoever shall say that men are justified by the mere imputation of Christ's righteousness, or by the mere remission of sins, exclusive of grace and charity which is shed abroad in their hearts by the Holy Spirit, and is inherent in them, or also, that the grace by which we are justified is only the favor of God, let him be anathema." Calvin replied: "I wish the reader to understand that as often as we mention Faith alone in this question, we are not thinking of a dead faith, which worketh not by love, but holding faith to be the only cause of justification. (Galatians 5:6; Romans 3:22.) It is therefore faith alone which justifies, and yet the faith which justifies is not alone: just as it is the heat alone of the sun which warms the earth, and yet in the sun it is not alone, because it is constantly conjoined with light."

[6] Matthew Henry, *Matthew Henry's Commentary on the Whole Bible*, (United States of America: Hendrickson Publishing, LLC, 1981).

[7] F. B. Meyer, *Tried by Fire: Expositions of the First Epistle of Peter*, (New York, NY: F. H. Revell, 1867).

[8] Deitrich Bonhoeffer, "*The Cost of Discipleship*," (New York, NY: Simon & Schuster, 1995).

[9] John R. W. Stott, "*The Message of Thessalonians 1 & 2*," The Bible Speaks Today Series, (Leicester, England: Inter-Varsity Press, 1991).

About the Author

Brenda has a heart and passion to serve women of all ages, sharing God's Word while encouraging them to be women after God's own heart.

As the wife of a retired Marine and retired Deputy Sheriff, she has a special place in her heart for those who serve in uniform.

Brenda has been writing since she was ten years old, first encouraged by her 5th grade English teacher. As a Christian author she has written devotionals, Women's Bible study curriculum, and is currently working on several book projects, being developed from her conference and retreat teachings.

She is available to teach Bible studies, conferences, retreats and writing workshops.

She loves to spend her free time in her favorite place - talking with God in her gardens. Brenda and her husband Jim live in beautiful Southern California. They have been married 28 years and have one daughter.

To contact Brenda, visit www.ineveryhand.org.

To order more copies of *One Tiny Seed*, please email Brenda at ineveryhand@gmail.com.